ADOPTABLE COPYRIGHT POLICY

COPYRIGHT INFORMATION BULLETIN SERIES

1. Jerome K. Miller, *Using Copyrighted Videocassettes in Classrooms and Libraries*, 1984 (out of print).

2. Charles W. Vlcek, *Copyright Policy Development: A Resource Book for Educators*, 1987.

3. Jerome K. Miller, *Using Copyrighted Videocassettes in Classrooms, Libraries, and Training Centers*, 2nd ed., 1987.

4. Esther R. Sinofsky, *A Copyright Primer for Educational and Industrial Media Producers*, 1988 (out of print).

5. Jerome K. Miller (Ed.), *Video Copyright Permissions: A Guide to Securing Permission to Retain, Perform, and Transmit Television Programs Videotaped Off the Air*, 1989.

6. Charles W. Vlcek, *Adoptable Copyright Policy: Copyright Policy and Manuals Designed For Adoption by Schools, Colleges & Universities*, 1992.

7. Leonard DuBoff, *High-tech Law (In Plain English®): An Entrepreneur's Guide*, 1991.

8. Ruth H. Dukelow, *The Library Copyright Guide*, 1992.

Available from:
Association for Educational Communications and Technology
1025 Vermont Avenue, NW, Suite 820
Washington, DC 20005

Adoptable Copyright Policy:

Copyright Policy and Manuals Designed For Adoption By Schools, Colleges & Universities

By

Dr. Charles W. Vlcek

COPYRIGHT INFORMATION SERVICES

COPYRIGHT INFORMATION SERVICES

An imprint of the
Association for Educational Communications and Technology
1025 Vermont Avenue, NW, Suite 820, Washington, DC 20005

Printed in the United States of America by
BookCrafters, Chelsea, Michigan

The Association for Educational Communications and Technology is an international professional association dedicated to the improvement of instruction through the effective use of media and technology. Periodicals, monographs, videotapes and audiotapes available through AECT meet the needs of media and learning resource specialists, educators, librarians, industrial trainers, and a variety of other educational technology professionals.

Table of Contents

Preface.. vii

About the Author... ix

Site License Information x

Part I: Adoptable Board Copyright Policy............................... 1

Part II: Adoptable Faculty Copyright Manual.......................... 5

Chapter 1: Overview... 7

Chapter 2: Applying the Law to Specific Media................. 21

Chapter 3: Copyright Management...................................... 45

Chapter 4: Copyright Quick Guide... 47

Chapter 5: Obtaining Permission............................... 57

Part III: Adoptable Student Copyright Manual.......................... 59

Appendices.. 63

Selected Bibliography... 111

Dedication

To those who must contend with

the obfuscated copyright law.

The opinions contained herein
reflect the author's informed opinion
but do not constitute legal advice.

Preface

Many educators urged me to write this adoptable Board Policy and Faculty Copyright Manual. Both are needed today to meet the complex responsibilities under the U.S. copyright law. The Board Policy (Part I of this book) was written to help school district, college and university boards establish a protective copyright policy. The model Board Policy was written for large or small institutions and can be modified to meet specific needs. It states the board's determination to observe the copyright law, establishes responsibility for infringements, informs the faculty that they must observe the law, and creates implementation and enforcement procedures.

The specifics of what, when, where and how employees may use copyrighted materials were deliberately excluded from the Board Policy to reduce the need for frequent policy changes. Instead, the details and procedures appear in the Faculty Copyright Manual (Part II of this book). As an administrative document, the manual can be changed to meet changing needs, without requiring board approval. The Faculty Copyright Manual restates the board policy and provides specific guidelines for many situations. Detailed explanations are purposely deleted, but footnotes direct readers to other sources.

Finally, a brief Student Copyright Manual appears in Part III. It was written to help students understand the purpose of the copyright law and its application to their studies.

To facilitate the implementation of this Board Policy, Faculty Copyright Manual, and Student Copyright Manual, the publisher agreed to publish them in both book and electronic format, with a license authorizing campus-wide, or district-wide duplication and distribution. If any of these documents are adopted by a multi-campus college or university, a multi-campus duplication and distribution license is available from the publisher for a modest price.

I hope I have succeeded in meeting your needs.

Charles W. Vlcek

About the Author

Charles W. Vlcek attended public schools in Eau Claire, Wisconsin and has bachelor and master degrees from the University of Wisconsin-Stout and an Ed.D. in Educational Media from Michigan State University.

He has been a high school teacher and media coordinator in the Milwaukee and Eau Claire, Wisconsin, public schools. He is presently Coordinator of Media Library Services and Professor of Instructional Media at Central Washington University. He has held consultantships in Singapore and Malaysia on media building design.

Dr. Vlcek has written extensively on instructional media and copyright and has been active in copyright discussions for the past twenty years. He serves as a copyright consultant, speaker and copyright workshop presenter extensively in the Pacific Northwest and nationally.

Site License Information

To facilitate the implementation of copyright policies in scools, colleges and other institutions, this book is also available in IBM-compatible computer disk format. The software is menu-driven to support major word processing programs so users can modify the manual to meet specific needs. Site license agreements for use of the electronic version are available to provide institutions the following rights:

1. To make and distribute copies of the computer disk for use within the institution;

2. To make and distribute paper copies from the computer disk for use within the institution;

3. To install the program for use in a local area network within the institution;

License Agreement Fee Structure
School District, college, or universities with enrollments:

a. Under 5000	$150
b. 5001 - 10,000	$300
c. 10,001 plus	$500

Available from:
The Association for Educational Communications & Technology
1025 Vermont Avenue, NW, Suite 820
Washington, DC 20005

Part I:

ADOPTABLE
BOARD COPYRIGHT POLICY

This copyright policy states the board's intention to observe the copyright law and establish procedures for managing copyright compliance. Every board member and administrator knows that law suits do occur. When they do, the institution, individual board members, and key administrators will probably be named in the suit. This policy places the burden of litigation where it belongs — on the individual(s) responsible for the illegal actions. If the board has a copyright policy in place, that is consistently supported by the administration, the institution, the board, and the administrators have an excellent chance to defend themselves and place the blame on the infringer(s). Failure to adopt and support a suitable copyright policy places the board in jeopardy if the institution is sued for copyright infringement due to the illegal actions of one employee.

COPYRIGHT POLICY

(Name of the Institution)

(Address)

This copyright policy was adopted by the (name of governing body) on (date) after review by (name and title of counsel).

1. It is the intent of the (name of governing body) that this (name of university, college, or school district) comply with the U.S. Copyright Law (Title 17, *U.S. Code*, Sect. 101, et seq.). This policy represents a sincere effort to observe the copyright law.

2. Employees are prohibited from copying copyrighted works unless the action is authorized by (a) specific exemptions in the copyright law, (b) the principle of fair use, (c) the fair-use guidelines, or d) licenses or written permission from the copyright owner. Any other copying must be approved by the institution's Copyright Officer on a case-by-case basis.

3. Employees are prohibited from "performing" copyrighted works unless the performance is authorized by (a) Title 17, *U.S. Code*, Sect. 110(1) (4) or (8), (b) performance licenses, (c) purchase order authorization, or (d) written permission from the copyright owner or the owner's agent.

4. The (title of the chief administrative officer) shall appoint a Copyright Officer who shall (a) implement this copyright policy, (b) prepare and distribute a Faculty Copyright Manual, (c) conduct training programs to assure that employees are aware of the copyright law, (d) answer questions about the copyright law, (e) maintain appropriate records of permissions, agreements, and licenses, (f) place appropriate copyright warning notices on or near copying equipment, and (g) other related duties, as needed.

5. Employees who willfully disregard the institution's Board Copyright Policy, or the specific provisions of the Faculty Copyright Manual, do so at their own risk and assume all liability, including the possibility of dismissal for persistent copyright infringements.

6. If the Copyright Officer is aware of copyright infringements by an employee, he/she shall counsel the infringer. If the employee continues to infringe the copyright law, the Copyright Officer shall inform the (title of the chief administrative officer) of the continuing infringements. The (title of the chief administrative officer) shall take appropriate steps to stop the illegal actions. If the infringer refuses to stop the infringements, the (title of the chief administrative officer) shall take appropriate steps to terminate the employment of the persistent infringer.

Adopted by

(name of governing body)

(name of institution)

(address)

(date)

Part II:

ADOPTABLE
FACULTY COPYRIGHT MANUAL

This Faculty Copyright Manual is a brief condensation of the law and the related legal documents. It is far too brief to completely encompass the law, but provides a brief summary of the points most likely to impact the faculty.

Chapter 1:

OVERVIEW

The U.S. Constitution gave Congress the power "To promote the progress of science and useful arts by securing for limited time to authors and inventors the exclusive right to their respective writings and discoveries."[1] The authors of the Constitution recognized that if the works of creators were not protected, it would undermine the incentive to create, and the dissemination of knowledge would be greatly curtailed. Congress passed the first national copyright act in 1790. Over 200 years, the copyright law has been completely revised five times and amended many more times, sometimes annually.

The last total revision of the copyright law passed in 1976 and went into effect on January 1, 1978.[2] It incorporated several major changes, (i.e., it extended the duration of copyright protection, expanded the scope of copyright, legislated a fair-use exemption, and addressed newer technologies).

What Can Be Copyrighted:

Copyright protection exists for all works created in any medium of expression as long as the works are fixed in a tangible medium of expression so they can be perceived or communicated with or without the aid of equipment.[3] These include:

1. Literary works;

2. Sheet music and musical performances;

3. Dramatic works, including any accompanying music;

4. Pantomimes and choreographic works;

5. Pictorial, graphic, and sculpture works;

6. Motion pictures and other audiovisual works; and

7. Sound recordings.[4]

Exclusive Rights:

The copyright law gives the copyright owner the exclusive right to do or to authorize the following:

1. "To reproduce the copyrighted work." The copyright owner has the exclusive right to publish or to withhold a work in any media. ·

2. "To prepare derivative works based upon the copyrighted work." Only the copyright owner may change, alter, or translate a work, or convert it to a new medium, or create a new work from an existing work.

3. "To distribute copies ... of the copyrighted work to the public by sale or other transfer of ownership, or by rental, lease, or lending." This exclusive right of "first publication" terminates with the "publication" of the work. Thereafter, the purchaser of a legitimate copy of a work may sell, lend, or dispose of the copy without the copyright owner's permission.

4. "In the case of literary, musical, dramatic and choreographic works, pantomimes, and motion pictures ... [and] other audiovisual works, the copyright owner has an exclusive right to "perform" (i.e., show) the copyrighted work publicly; and"

5. "In the case of literary, musical, dramatic and choreographic works, pantomimes and pictorial, graphic or sculptural works, including individual images of a motion picture or other audiovisual work, the copyright owner has an exclusive right to display the copyrighted work publicly."[5]

Copyright Registration:

A work is automatically protected the moment it is created in a tangible medium of expression. However, this right cannot be enforced until the work is registered at the U.S. Copyright Office. To be eligible for copyright protection, works must be original and represent appreciable creativity.[6] Unpublished works may be registered anytime within the term of copyright protection. Copyright notices are not required on works published after March 1, 1989.[7] However, if a work is published after that date, one must assume it is copyrighted. Authors, artists, and producers are still urged to place a copyright notice on all creative works, and to register their copyrights promptly to establish a public record of ownership.

Duration of Copyright:

Copyright protection under the 1909 law was twenty-eight years, renewable for another twenty-eight years, for a total of fifty-six years. Works created after January 1, 1978 are protected for the life of the author, plus fifty years.[8] Protection for multi-authored works, extends to the life of the longest-lived author, plus fifty years.[9] Anonymous and pseudonymous works and work made for hire are protected for seventy-five years from first publication.[10] For works in their second term of copyright registration under the 1909 law, the protection extends to seventy-five years from the date of publication or creation.[11] For works in their first term of protection under the 1909 law, the registration is extended to seventy-five years by renewing the registration in the twenty-eighth year.[12] All copyrights expire on December thirty-first of the last year of protection.[13]

Figure 1: Copyright Duration Table

Date of Creation or Publication	End of First-term Protection	End of Protection if Registration was Renewed
	(28 Years)	(75 Years)
1910	1938	1985
1920	1948	1995
1930	1958	2005
1940	1968	2015
1950	1978	2025

Works Made For Hire:

Works "made for hire" are protected for seventy-five years from the year of creation or publication or one hundred years from the day the work was created, whichever comes first.[14] These include works created by an employee as part of his or her job where the copyright is held by the employer. It also includes works made by independent contractors who transfer the copyright by means of employment contracts. Many universities, colleges and schools have service contracts which specify the assignment of copyright ownership and the division of royalties for works created by the faculty. These contracts frequently only apply only to works created using institutional facilities or staff.

Unpublished Works:

Many works are never published but they are protected from the moment of creation. These works include diaries, correspondence, notes, sketches, photographs, recordings, films, videos, etc. They are fully protected without a copyright notice or copyright registration. Unpublished works created prior to January 1, 1978 are protected until December 31, 2002; those created after January 1, 1978 are protected for the life of the creator, plus fifty years. The creator of unpublished works has the same "right of first publication" as published works which gives him or her the control of the use of the work. Unpublished works may not be duplicated except for purposes of preservation, security, or deposit in another library for research.[15]

Public Domain:

Copyrighted materials enter the public domain when copyright protection expires. Works published before January 1, 1978 without a proper copyright notice entered the public domain immediately upon publication. Works remain in the public domain even when re-published in a new copyrighted work. Works which are in the public domain may be used without permission.

Works created by employees of the U.S. government while performing their official duties are in the public domain.[16] However, some government works are protected if:

(1) The copyright has been transferred to the government as a gift;[17]

(2) The work was created by a grantee who was permitted to claim a copyright in the work;[18]

11

(3) A privately-created copyrighted work is included in a government document.[19]

Performing Rights:

One of the exclusive rights given to the copyright holder is the right to control performances of all copyrighted works. (This includes the right to control showing of audiovisual works.) Section 110(1) of the copyright law provides a limited exemption to that right. Teachers and pupils may perform (show) copyrighted works in the classroom. The exception requires that the performance be carried out by instructors or students in a nonprofit institution in a classroom or similar place of instruction (i.e., laboratory, auditorium, gymnasium, or library). The exemption only applies to performances in face-to-face instruction in a course given for academic credit. It does not cover performances for entertainment or recreational purposes as a part of lunchhour, recess, or after-school activities. It also does not authorize performing works in common rooms of student housing. "Nontheatrical public performance licenses" are required to perform audiovisual works in those circumstances or locations. Performing dramatic works requires an appropriate license from the playwrights' agent.[20]

Fair Use:

While the copyright law gave authors the exclusive right to their works, the law also provides some limitations to those rights. The theory of fair use was developed by the courts as a "rule of reason" to assist in deciding court cases. This judicial "rule of reason" was incorporated in statutory copyright law by the Copyright Revision Act of 1976. (Full text in Appendix K, Sect. 107.) The law offers four broad criteria for applying fair use.

"1. The purpose and character of the use, including whether it is for commercial or nonprofit education purposes;"

This addresses the issue of how the material is used and by whom. Fair use has some application to reproducing copyrighted works for educational purposes, in nonprofit educational institution.

"2. The nature of the copyrighted work;"

Fair-use guidelines have been developed for three groups of materials, (i.e., print materials, music, and television). The type of material must be considered and the appropriate fair use guidelines must be applied. Congress specified that certain types of materials should rarely be copied; they are identified later in this manual.

"3. The amount and substantiality of the portion used in relation to the work as a whole;"

Fair-use guidelines are available for copying parts of books and sheet music. For other materials the smaller the amount that is copied, the more likely it is that the action is a fair use. Copying up to ten percent of a work is usually considered safe, except when the parts copied are crucial to the whole material, or if they are rare or difficult to create.

"4. The effect of the use on the potential market for or value of the work."[21]

Effect can be measured in competing and non-competing uses:

Competing Uses:

Uses that deprive the creator of a sale, lease or rental are probably not a fair use. (These include duplicating print, audio, and video materials instead of purchasing, renting, leasing, or licensing additional copies).

13

Non-competing Uses:

Non-competing uses do not adversely affect the copyright owner. For example, making two slides from a magazine for classroom use when the slides are not commercially available, duplicating materials which are not available for sale, rental, lease, or licensing, etc. may not affect the copyright owner. Fair use has greater application to non-competing uses, but repeated copying may still be illegal.

Fair-Use Guidelines:

Although the four fair-use criteria are written into the law, it is not always clear when they are met. Congress asked the Register of Copyrights to develop specific educational guidelines for interpreting the fair-use criteria. Three groups met to develop fair-use guidelines for duplicating (1) print materials, (2) sheet music, and (3) television programs. The guidelines were ratified by Congress as an expression of the "intent" of the legislature. The committees that wrote the guidelines included representatives of educators, authors, publishers, studios, and labor unions. While the guidelines were not endorsed by all the groups involved, they have been ratified by Congress and will be considered in court cases involving infringements by educators. For this reason, they must be viewed as valid guidelines. The guidelines may change as the law evolves through court cases, but, at present, they seem to offer suitable direction to educators. The fair-use guidelines will be discussed later in the treatment of each type of material.

Copyright Warning Notices:

The law specifies that copyright warning notices shall be posted at the place where library or archives employees accept orders for copies. The text of the following notice is specified by federal regulation.[23]

NOTICE

Warning concerning copyright restrictions. The copyright Law Of The United States (Title 17, *United States Code*) governs the making of photocopies or other reproductions of copyrighted material.

Under certain conditions specified in the law, libraries and archives are authorized to furnish a photocopy or other reproduction. One of these specified conditions is that the photocopy or reproduction is not to be used for any purpose other than private study, scholarship, or research. If a user makes a request for, or later uses a photocopy or reproduction for purposes in excess of fair use, that user may be liable for copyright infringement.

This institution reserves the right to refuse to accept a copying order if, in its judgment, fulfillment of the order would involve violation of the law.

A notice also must be displayed on or near all library or archival equipment capable of duplicating copyrighted materials and must be visible to anyone using the device.[22] Copying equipment includes photocopying machines, mimeograph machines, transparency markers, audio and video recorders, photographic copy stands, microfilm printers, and computers. It is desirable to place copyright warning notices at places where patrons borrow equipment for removal from the premises. Although the law only requires warning notices on equipment in libraries and archives, it is prudent to include them on or near all copying equipment used by faculty, staff, and students. The following notice is recommended by the American Library Association. [24]

> NOTICE: The copyright law of the United States (Title 17, *U.S. Code*) governs the making of copies of copyrighted materials. The person using this equipment is liable for any infringement.

Libraries and archives also are required to place a copyright warning notice on the first page of copies they make

> NOTICE: This material may be protected by copyright law (Title 17, *U.S. Code*).

for patrons. The notice recommended by the American Library Association reads:[25]

Penalties for Infringement:

A copyright infringer can be liable for actual damages and profits, or for statutory damages, as determined by a court. Statutory damages range from $250 to $50,000 per infringement, depending upon the extent of the infringement.[26] (An amendment is being considered which will increase the penalties.) In addition, the infringer can be assessed for court costs and the plaintiff's attorney's fees. Court costs and attorney's fees frequently exceed the amount of damages and profits. When infringements are made for profit, criminal charges and potential imprisonment may be added.

Innocent Infringers:

An innocent infringer is one who can convince a court that he or she did not know their actions were an infringement of the law. In these cases, the statutory damages can be lowered to not less than $100.[27] Any faculty member who received this Faculty

Copyright Manual would have great difficulty proving he or she was an innocent infringer.

Contributory Infringers:

Contributory infringers are persons who have knowledge of infringing activities, but do nothing about it. A librarian, media coordinator, dean, or principal who knows about an infringement, (e.g., television programs videotaped off the air which are retained longer than permitted by the fair-use guidelines), and who does nothing about it, is a contributory infringer. He or she is likely to be named in litigation. When a copyright owner files a formal complaint against an institution for an infringement, those named in the complaint usually include the the members of the governing board, the chief executive officer, the infringer(s), and contributory infringers.

Sovereign Immunity

Under the Eleventh Amendment to the Constitution, tax-supported agencies were not liable for copyright infringements. The issue was tested when B.V. Engineering, a small firm, provided the University of California at Los Angeles with engineering software on a test basis. UCLA made copies and returned the original to B.V. Engineering without purchasing the software. In the resulting case. *B.V. Engineering v. The University of California at Los Angeles*, the Supreme Court held that the university was not liable because of the protection offered by the Eleventh Amendment.[28] In a more recent case, *Anderson v. Radford University*, the Supreme Court held the university immune from liability, but Deborah Brown, a university employee, was not immune from liability for copyright infringements or violations of contractual agreements.[29]

Congress closed the sovereign immunity loophole by passing the Copyright Remedy Clarification Act on October 26,

17

1990.[30] The Act permits tax-supported agencies and their employees to be sued for copyright infringements. The Eleventh Amendment, can no longer be used as a legal defense for copyright infringements by tax-supported agencies.

REFERENCES

[1]*U.S. Constitution.* Article 1, Section 8

[2]Title 17, *U.S. Code.* Hereafter cited as "Copyright Act."

[3]Copyright Act, Section 102(a)

[4]Copyright Act, Section 102(a)

[5]Copyright Act, Section 106(5)

[6]Copyright Act, Section 106

[7]*Copyright Basics*, Circular 1, Washington D.C.: U.S. Government Printing Office, June 1989

[8]Copyright Act, Section 302(a)

[9]Copyright Act, Section 302(b)

[10]Copyright Act, Section 302(c)

[11]Copyright Act, Section 304(b)

[12]Copyright Act, Section 304(b)

[13]Copyright Act, Section 305

[14]Copyright Act, Section 302(c)

[15]Copyright Act, Section 108(b)

[16]Copyright Act, Section 105

[17]Ibid.

[18]*House Report,* No. 94-1476, 94th Congress, 2nd Session (1976), p. 59

[19]Ibid., p. 60

[20]Copyright Act, Section 110(1); and relevant passages in House and Senate Reports

[21]Copyright Act, Section 107

[22]Copyright Act, Section 108(d)(s) and (e)(2)

[23]*Federal Register* (42 Fed. Reg. 59264), November 16, 1977, pp 59264-5

[24]"Three Words Added to Copyright Notice" *American Libraries* 9, No. 1 (January, 1978), p. 22

[25]"Warning Notices for Copies and Machines," *American Libraries* 8, No. 10 (November, 1977), p. 530

[26]Copyright Act, Section 504(2)

[27]Copyright Act, Section 504(2)(c)

[28]*B.V. Engineering v. The University of California at Los Angeles.* U.S. Supreme Court (109SCt, 1557, 103LEd2d 859.)

[29] *Richard Anderson Photography v. Deborah Brown and Radford University.* U.S. Spreme Court (109SCt 1171, 103LEd2d), 229.

[30]Copyright Remedy Clarification Act, Public Law 101-553, November 15, 1990.

Chapter 2:

APPLYING THE LAW TO SPECIFIC MEDIA

This chapter provides a brief synopsis of the law as it applies to commonly-used media.

PRINT MATERIALS

"Print materials" include books, periodicals, pamphlets, newspapers and similar items. This discussion is limited to copying by or for the faculty, as student and library photocopying is treated elsewhere. The fair-use section of the copyright law authorizes individuals to copy a small part of a work. The fair-use section of the copyright law is interpreted by the "Agreement on Guidelines for Classroom Copying in Not for Profit Educational Institutions with Respect to Books and Periodicals." It was developed at the request of Congress by representatives of the Authors League of America, the Association of American Publishers, and the Ad Hoc Committee of Educational Institutions and Organizations on Copyright Law Revision.[1] The guidelines apply to teaching and research in nonprofit educational institutions. The full text appears in Appendix A and is summarized as follows:

1. Single Copying by Teachers:

The following are *minimum* statements of fair use:

A teacher may make a single copy of any of the following for his or her research, lesson preparation, or use in teaching:

    a. A chapter of a book;

    b. An article from a periodical or newspaper;

    c. A short story, short essay or short poem;

    d. A chart, graph, diagram, cartoon or picture from a book, periodical, or newspaper. More then one illustration can be copied if they are included in a chapter or article being copied.

2. Multiple Copies for Classroom Use:

The following are *minimum* statements of fair use:

One copy can be made for each student in a class when the following conditions are met:

    a. Poetry: a complete poem if it is less than 250 words and printed on not more than two pages, or an excerpt of not more than 250 words.

    b. Prose: (1) a complete article, story or essay if it is less than 2,500 words, or (2) an excerpt not to exceed 1,000 words or ten percent of the work, whichever is less. When ten percent of the work is less than 500 words, a minimum of 500 words may be used.

c. Charts, graphs, diagrams, drawings, cartoons, and pictures: One chart, graph, diagram, drawing, cartoon or picture per book or per periodical issue if the individual item is not separately copyrighted. More than one of each may be copied if they are included and meet the criteria in 2(b)(2), above.

d. Special works. These include children's picture books and comic books which combine illustrations with a limited text. These works usually have less than 2,500 words in their entirety. Copying these works is limited to two pages, on condition that those two pages do not include more than ten percent of the words in the work.

e. Each copy includes a copyright warning notice, previously described.

f. The copying must be at the request or inspiration of the individual teacher.

g. The inspiration to use a material and the time when needed for use does not allow purchasing or seeking permission. This requirement disallows repeated use at a later date.

h. The copies are to be used only in one course in the school. A "course" appears to include multi-section courses taught by the same or different teachers as one course using a uniform text and lesson plan. In colleges and universities, a course ends at the conclusion of each academic term. In elementary and secondary schools, it usually stops at the end of a grading period.

i. Not more than one poem, article, story, essay or two excerpts may be copied from one author, or more then three from a work or periodical volume (as opposed to an issue) during one class term.

j. Not more than nine items from all sources may be multiple copied for one course during one class term. This restriction does not apply to current news periodicals and public domain materials.

3. Prohibitions to 1 and 2, above:

a. Copying may not be used to create anthologies, compilations or collective works.

b. "Consumable works" (i.e., workbooks, exercises, test booklets, etc.) may not be copied.

c. Copying shall not (1) substitute for purchases, (2) be directed by higher authority, or (3) be repeated by the same teacher without permission from the copyright owner.

d. The copies shall be distributed free, or the copying charges shall be limited to the actual cost of copying.

Copying by a Library or Archives:

Section 108 of the copyright act gives nonprofit libraries and archives considerable latitude in what they can copy. This copying is separate from fair-use copying, treated earlier. The copyright law, permits libraries and archives to make single copies for patrons without permission and multiple copies for patrons when certain conditions are met. The law also authorizes duplicating certain non-print materials.

Libraries and archives must meet certain basic requirements to employ this exception:

1. All copies must be made without direct or indirect commercial advantage;

2. The collections of the library or archives must be open to the public. In the case of limited-access research libraries, the collection must be open to qualified researchers regardless of their occupational or professional affiliation;

3. All photocopies must display a copyright warning notice on the first page of the photocopy. (See Copyright Warning Notices in Chapter 1.);

4. All copies must become the property of the patron;

5. The library or archives must not be aware that a copy made for a patron will be used for any purpose other than private study, scholarship, or research; and

6. The library or archives must display a copyright warning notice at the place where it accepts orders for copies, and on its interlibrary loan request forms (See Copyright Warning Notices in Chapter 1).[2]

Copying for Patrons:

A library meeting the above conditions may copy:

1. A single journal article or a small part of a book, or other copyrighted work.

2. A library or archives may reproduce for a patron an entire copyrighted work, or a substantial part of it, if the library determined, after a reasonable investigation, that a new or used copy cannot be obtained at a fair price.[3]

The library photocopying section of the law does not extend to musical, pictorial, graphic or sculptural works except for illustrations appearing in a book or periodical which may be copied as a part of the article or section being copied.[4] Fair use permits copying some of these works by a library or archives if

25

the user requests the copy for legitimate scholarship, research, or teaching purposes (See Fair Use in Chapter 1).

Section 108 allows a library or archives to record, duplicate, retain and lend a limited number of copies and excerpts of television news programs. News programs include actual news reports but exclude news analysis and news-magazine programs. No other audiovisual materials may be copied under the library photocopying section of the law. News programs copied under this provision may only be used in research and not in teaching.[5]

Copying for its own collection or for the collections of another library or archives; libraries and archives may reproduce one copy of a work for their own collections or for those of another library or archives under the following conditions:

1. A library or archives may reproduce in facsimile form (e.g., photocopy or microform) any unpublished work currently in its collection. The copy must be made for the preservation and security of the original or for deposit for research use in another library or archives.[6]

2. A library may make a replacement copy of a published work in its own collection if the original is damaged, deteriorated, lost, or stolen. (Copies may not be made in anticipation that they may be "damaged, deteriorated, lost, or stolen.") The copy can be made from a work in its own collection or from a copy in another library or archives. Before making the copy, the library or archives must make a reasonable effort to find an unused replacement copy at a fair price.[7]

Interlibrary Loans:

Libraries may make copies of materials for sharing with other libraries through interlibrary loan.[8] Interlibrary loan copying is governed by guidelines developed by the National Commission on New Technological Uses of Copyright Works (CONTU). The complete text appears in Appendix E and is summarized here:

1. A library may request no more than five copies of articles from a periodical volume (not an issue) per year. However, this limitation does not apply to articles published five or more years before the date of the request.

2. A library or archives may request no more than five excerpts from a book or pamphlet while it is subject to copyright protection. (See the table of copyright expiration dates on page 14.)

3. The above limitations do not apply, if:

   a. The library has ordered a subscription to the periodical, or

   b. The library owns the work but the copy is lost, stolen, or otherwise unavailable when the reproduction is requested, or

   c. The library has ordered the title, but it has not arrived.

Under any of these circumstances, the requesting library or archives may request a copy through interlibrary loan as a fair use, but the request does not count as one of the five copies authorized by the CONTU guidelines.

4. Interlibrary loan requests must state that the request conforms with the CONTU guidelines or other provisions of the copyright law. Copies made under item 3, above, fall under the "other provisions" section of the guidelines.

5. The requesting library must maintain records of filled orders. The records must be retained for three years after the end of the calendar year.[9]

Library Reserve:

Single or multiple copies of periodical articles and chapters of books may be placed on reserve in a library under the terms of Section 107, on fair use.[10] A single copy may be the faculty member's single, fair-use copy. Multiple copies may be placed on reserve in lieu of distributing multiple copies of the item to students in the class. The amount of copying under this exemption must be restricted to the number of items that may be distributed to a class during a term. Copies made under this provision only may be used for the semester in which they were placed on reserve. Any further use of the copies requires the permission of the copyright owner. The number of copies placed on reserve must be limited to a "reasonable" number. This obviously depends upon the size of the class; one copy per ten students may be "reasonable," but the American Library Association (ALA) and American Association of Law Librarians (AALL) suggest a limit of six copies, regardless of the number enrolled.[11]

In summary, copying material for reserve purposes should meet the following conditions:

1. The faculty member's single, fair-use copy, or

2. Multiple copies placed on reserve which conform to the limits in the "Agreement on Guidelines for Classroom Copying...." The quantity placed on reserve shall be "reasonable" in relation to the number of students in the class.

3. The copy(s) on reserve shall be identified as belonging to a faculty member and include a copyright notice or a copyright warning notice, or both.

4. Copying the material shall not adversely effect the market for the work.

5. Photocopied material may not be revised in subsequent semesters without the copyright owner's permission.

MUSIC

Separate copyrights usually exist for sheet music and recorded musical performance. Additional copyrights may exist in the lyrics. Composers, lyricists, arrangers, performers, etc. receive royalties from the sale of their creative works. Music dealers usually sell sheet music in sets (e.g., band sets, chorus sets, etc.). Single copies may not be available from dealers but can be ordered directly from the publisher. Copying sheet music without permission deprives the composers of royalties. Copying recordings deprives composers, arrangers, performers, etc. of their royalties. Fair-use guidelines for music were developed by the Music Publishers' Association, the National Music Publishers' Association, the Music Educators' National Conference, the National Association of Schools of Music, and the Ad Hoc Committee on Copyright Law Revision. The guidelines authorize limited copying and altering of sheet music. They also authorize recording student performances. The guidelines appear in Appendix B and are summarized here:

Fair-Use Guidelines for Music:

  1. Copying Sheet Music:

  A. Emergency copies may be made to replace lost music when time does not permit purchasing replacement music before a performance. The emergency copies must be destroyed at the end of the performance and replaced with purchased copies.

  B. For teaching purposes, not performance, multiple copies of excerpts may be made provided that the excerpts do not constitute a performable unit such as a section, movement, or aria. The excerpt may not be larger than ten percent of the whole work and not more then one copy per pupil may be made.

  C. For teaching purposes, not for a performance, a single copy of an entire performable unit (section, movement, aria, etc.) that is confirmed by the copyright proprietor to be out of print or unavailable except in a larger work, may be made for a teacher for his or her scholarly research or preparation to teach a class.

  D. Purchased sheet music may be edited or simplified if the fundamental character of the work is not distorted. Lyrics may not be altered or added if none exist.[12]

  2. Musical Recordings:

  A. Student performances may be recorded for evaluation purposes only. The recording may be retained by the institution or the teacher.

  B. At one point, the committee included a provision authorizing educators to reproduce sound recordings owned by an education institution or an individual teacher for the purpose of constructing aural learning exercises or examinations. This provision was withdrawn just before the guidelines were approved by Congress. Transfers from disk to tape or disk to cassette always require permission.

3. Performances:

A. As discussed above, the fair-use guidelines allow student performance to be recorded if the recordings are made only for critique or evaluation. That same privilege does not extend to recording performances by professional musicians from outside the institution without the permission of the performer **and** the copyright owner of the music. Licenses must be obtained for all public performances, unless they fall under the "free and benefit" provisions discussed below.

B. Live public performances of non-theatrical musical works are authorized under the "free and benefit" performance provision in Section 110(4) of the copyright law. (Full text in Appendix K, Sect. 110.) The performance must be given without charge to the audience, or the income from admission fees in excess of costs must be applied to a charitable cause. In either case, the managers and performers must contribute their services or their contribution to the performance must be part of their overall duties as faculty members or staff members.[13] This appears to authorize musical performances at school athletic events, if the proceeds over costs are applied to a charitable cause, such as a scholarship fund. In practice, most colleges and universities purchase performance licenses from the three major musical licensing agencies listed in Appendix J. These licenses cover all student performances of non-dramatic musical works. As a result of an "understanding" between the attorney for a major educational association and the licensing agencies, the agencies do not sell licenses to school districts.

C. Recorded music may not be performed at social occasions without a license from the licensing agencies listed in Appendix J.

4. Copying Records:

Copyrighted musical recordings may not be copied without permission. Such permission is rarely granted, so educators have little choice except to purchase additional quantities of the recordings.

5. Musical Transmissions and Broadcasts:

Live or recorded music may not be transmitted through a multi-room public-address system or cable system without a license. Live or recorded music may not be broadcast unless the station holds licenses from the three music licensing services listed in Appendix J.

TELEVISION PROGRAMS

1. Off-air and Cable Receptions:

Television broadcasts and cable transmissions may be received and simultaneously shown to classes.

2. Recording Commercial Television Programs at School:

Commercial television programs for classroom use fall under the terms of guidelines. Guidelines were developed by representatives of educational organizations, copyright proprietors and creative guilds (unions). While some proprietors disagree with the guidelines, the guidelines will impact any litigation involving videotaping off the air for classroom use. The text of the guidelines appears in Appendix C and are summarized here:

A. The guidelines only apply to off-air recording by nonprofit educational organizations.

B. Programs may be recorded from broadcast transmissions or from a simultaneous retransmission by cable distribution systems.

C. Programs must be transmitted to the general public without charge. This eliminates "pay" programming, (i.e., HBO, CineMax, Disney Channel, etc.).

D. Programs may be retained for forty-five calendar days from date of recording. After forty-five days they must be erased or permission must be obtained for continued retention and use.

E. Programs may be shown to a class once, and repeated once for reinforcement, during the first ten "teaching days" following the broadcast. A "teaching day" is a day on which pupils receive instruction. It excludes holidays, weekends, examination periods and other non-teaching days.

F. Off-air recordings may be made by the teacher or by a media specialist or librarian at the request of a teacher. Programs may not be re-recorded by or for the same teacher when they are rebroadcast.

G. Programs may not be recorded in anticipation of teacher requests.

H. Off-air recordings need not be used in their entirety but they may not be altered from their original content, or electronically combined or merged.

I. All copies of off-air recordings must include the copyright notice, if one appeared in the program.

J. Educational institutions are expected to establish appropriate control procedures.[14] An appropriate form appears in Appendix I.

3. Recording Commercial Television Programs at Home for Classroom Use:

There has been some concern about recording programs in the teachers' homes and using the recordings in classrooms. The Sony Betamax case established that recording in the home for the use of the family and its friends was permissible. It did not address the issue of teachers or students bringing the recorded programs to school for classroom viewing. There is a general consensus that bringing programs recorded at home to school for classroom viewing is permissible if the recording and performances comply with the "Guidelines for Off-Air Recording of Broadcast Programming for Educational Purposes." It also should be emphasized that using programs beyond the ten "teaching day" limit is a copyright infringement.

4. Recording Television Programs Off the Satellite:

Satellite programming is protected by the Federal Communications Act.[15] Basically, programming may not be received without a license or written permission. The fair-use exemptions in the copyright law does not apply, as satellite transmissions are private communications protected by the Federal Communications Act. A recent amendment to the Federal Communications Act authorizes "private viewing" in the home, if:

A. The programming is listed as "free" in a reputable satellite programming directory.

B. The programs are not scrambled or a subscription service has not been established. [16]

This exemption applies only to viewing in the home and does not apply to educational receptions. An increasing number of educational satellite programs are now available, (i.e., the Learning Channel, International University Consortium, National Technological University, PBS Adult Learning Satellite Service, etc.). These programs are offered through membership or by contract. Reception without a license or membership is illegal.

5. Recording Public Broadcasting Service (PBS) Programs:

Most PBS series are produced by a consortium of stations that underwrite the series and a producer who produces and distributes the series. The agreement between the stations and the producer frequently includes a provision authorizing the viewers of the underwriting stations to record and reuse the programs. The terms of these agreements vary widely and many European producers and distributors do not grant educational duplication rights. Since these rights vary from station to station, contact your local PBS station(s) for duplication rights.

6. Cable Transmission of Audiovisual Works:

Cable "transmission" of copyrighted works is limited to non-dramatic literary works.[17] Because audiovisual works are excluded from the definition of literary works, audiovisual works may not be transmitted without a license.[18] Many video distributors give free, in-building transmission licenses, but sell licenses for multi-building transmissions. Licenses are available from most educational video distributors and the prices are often negotiable. Cable transmission rights can and should be specified in institutional purchase orders for audiovisual materials so the transmission right is acquired simultaneously with the purchase of the programs.[19]

7. Home-Use-Only and Rental-Store Videos:

Questions have been raised about the legality of classroom showings of videos labeled "For Home Use Only." Videos are sold with and without "nontheatrical-public-performance rights." Those sold with the rights usually cost more because of the additional value conveyed in the sale. Videos rented or sold at neighborhood video stores or sold through mail-order catalogs are offered without performance rights, so they are labeled "For Home Use Only," or something similar. Since they are sold without a performance license they are intended for private viewing in homes limited to family and friends. These videos are usually much cheaper than videos sold with a performance license. Some educational media distributors sell their products with or without "nontheatrical-public-performance rights." Other firms only sell films and videos without licenses.

One trade association operates a public relations campaign to persuade educators that it is illegal to show "For Home Use Only" videos in classrooms. However, Section 110(1) of the copyright law states explicitly that any legitimately-made, copyrighted work may be performed or displayed by "instructors or pupils," in "face to face teaching activities," in "nonprofit educational institutions," in "classrooms or similar places devoted to teaching." Outside of that trade association, there is a general consensus that Section 110(1) allows showing videocassettes labeled "For Home Use Only" in classrooms when the following conditions are met:

A. They must be shown only to teachers and students in face-to-face instruction,

B. They must be shown only in courses given for academic credit,

C. They must be shown only in classrooms or other locations devoted to instruction (e.g. laboratories, gymnasiums, libraries, etc.), and

D. They must be legitimately-made copies.

Videocassettes labeled "For Home Use Only" may not be shown under the following circumstances:

A. Showings during entertainment or recreation activities (e.g. recess, lunch-hour, and after-school showings),

B. Showings to an audience which is not confined to the students and faculty assigned to a specific course, (e.g., showings at parents' programs, residence-hall social gathering, or community activities), and

C. Showings from illegally-made copies.[20]

COMPUTER SOFTWARE

The 1976 copyright law was deliberately vague about copyright protection for computer software until a congressional committee could complete a study. The law was amended on December 12, 1980, following the receipt of the committee report. The amendment defines computer software as a literary work, which gives software copyright protection immediately upon creation. The amendment also permitted making one archival or back-up copy of each program.[21] The International Council for Computers in Education (ICCE) issues a "Suggested Policy Statement on Duplicating and Using Computer Software in Academic Settings." The latest edition of that statement appears in Appendix D and is summarized here:

Back-up Copy:

The Copyright Act allows the purchaser of software to:

1. Make one copy of software for archival purposes in case the original is destroyed or damaged through mechanical failure

of a computer. However, if the original is sold or given away, the archival copy must be destroyed.

2. Make necessary adaptations to use the program.

3. Add features to the program for specific applications. These improvements may not be sold or given away without the copyright owner's permission.

Computer Laboratories:

In computer laboratories where students and teachers have access to software, the institution should establish procedures that prevent illegal copying of software. Appropriate warning notices should be posted at the supervisor's desk or the sign-in station. A suggested warning notice follows:

SOFTWARE COPYING WARNING

Software is protected by the copyright law and may not be copied without the copyright owner's permission. You are liable for damages resulting from illegal duplication of software.

A short warning notice also should appear on all sign-in or check-out forms. (The form appears on the following page.)

Multiple Loading:

It is convenient to load one program disk into several computers for simultaneous use of the program. It is unclear if this is legal, but the ICCE Software Guidelines suggest that this should not be allowed. Licenses authorizing multiple loading are available from some publishers.

COMPUTER USER AGREEMENT FORM

As a condition of using the institutions computer equipment, I agree not to use the equipment to duplicate copyrighted software, whether it is my personal copy or is owned by the institution. I assume liability for any copyright infringements caused by me.

Signed:_____ Date:_____

Networks:

Many educational institutions have local-area networks (LAN) or wide-area networks (WAN) which enable large computers to serve many smaller computers or terminals within the institution. Licenses are required to use software on networks.[22]

Database Downloading:

Downloading involves copying a data transmission from database utility to a user's computer. This shortens the "connect time," which is the basis for most user fees. It also enables the searcher to clean up the data before printing a copy. Databases are copyrightable and copying from a database to a computer appears to be a copyright infringement. The copyright owners generally accept temporary downloading as a fair use as long as only one report is printed and the data is erased after printing the report. The problem centers on long-term retention of data to reuse or to combine to create a local database. Long-term retention for any purpose requires a downloading license. These licenses are offered by most database utilities.[23]

OTHER ISSUES

Films and Videotapes:

Films and videotapes may not be copied or altered unless the copying meets the four tests for fair use. While no guidelines have been developed, copying a small part of a film or videotape may be permissible, if the four fair-use criteria are met. Producers argue that some parts of a program are critical to the total program and copying even a small part violates the "substantiality" test in the second fair-use criterion. The courts have not established the validity of that argument or the amount of copying required to be "substantial," so caution is recommended.

Copying or altering an entire film or video without written permission is clearly an infringement, unless it can be documented that the copy was made to preserve an old program that is no longer available. Copying "preview" prints for any reason is a conspicuous copyright infringement.

Filmstrips and Slide Sets:

Copying filmstrips and slide sets in their entirety, or altering a program, requires written permission. Transferring a program to another format, (i.e., filmstrip to video, or filmstrip to slides) also requires permission. Copying a few frames or slides may be a fair use, if the four fair-use criteria are met.

Microforms:

Microforms (microfilms, microfiche, etc.) are protected under the copyright act. The rules governing microforms are determined by the nature of the work contained therein, (i.e., a literary work, graphic work, etc.). Microform copies of old books, periodicals, and manuscripts may be copied freely if the original works are in the public domain. If the original publication is copyrighted, copies may be made using the rules that apply to books and periodicals.

Newsletters:

Newsletters are unique because they are very brief and have a small circulation. Therefore, almost any copying deprives the publisher of a sale or subscription. Limited copying is possible under the "small part" exemption in the library photocopying or fair-use sections of the law. However, a small part of a four-page newsletter may consist of only a few lines of text. Copying newsletters must be approached with great caution.

Artworks:

Artworks are copyrightable. The duplication of such works, in their entirety by photography, sketching, rendering, casting, or printing are violations of the copyright law. The only exception is for copying illustrations in a book or periodical under the terms of "Agreement on Guidelines for Classroom Copying" or the library photocopying section of the law.

Electrocopying (Computer Scanning):

Electrocopying is the process of entering books, periodicals, artworks, etc. into a computer by means of an optical scanner. Once a work is entered in the computer, it can be edited, manipulated, and reproduced. Electrocopying a text may be a fair use if it is used only for research, (e.g., for textual analysis). Any other electrocopying of copyrighted texts requires the permission of the copyright owner. Artworks should not be electrocopied without permission, unless they are in the public domain. Electrocopying by students as a "learning exrcise" may be permissible but the copies should be promptly erased.

Dramatic Works:

The right of the copyright owner to perform a dramatic work publicly, precludes all public performance of a play, opera, operetta, or musical comedy without a license.[24] Dramatic works may be performed in the classroom under the Section 110(1) exception, but all the requirements of that exception must be met, including the requirement that attendance be limited to the teacher and the pupils enrolled in the course.[25]

Student Projects:

While the law does not specifically address student uses of copyrighted works, the Senate Report accompanying the Copyright Revision Act of 1976 identifies "special uses" by students:

> There are certain classroom uses which, because of their special nature, would not be considered an infringement in the ordinary case. For example, copying of extracts by pupils as exercises in a shorthand or typing class or for foreign language study ... Likewise, a single reproduction of excerpts from a copyrighted work by a student calligrapher .... in a learning situation would be a fair use of the copyrighted work.[26]

Based upon that statement, a consensus has developed that students may copy copyrighted works as a learning exercise. This suggests that students can integrate all types of materials into sound/slide, film, or television productions. Programs made under this exemption may be submitted to the teacher for a grade, and may be shown to the other students in the class. However, the paper or product must remain the property of the student. Copies may not be retained by the teacher or the institution, it may not be shown, transmitted, or broadcast outside the classroom, and no copies may be sold or given away. Students who wish to make copies beyond these narrow constraints, or who wish to make additional uses of their student projects must use the permission procedures identified in Chapter 5. (See also Part III, the Student Copyright Manual.)

REFERENCES

[1] Composed of representatives from forty-one educational and professional organizations

[2] Copyright Act, Section 108

[3] Copyright Act, Section 108(e)

[4] Copyright Act, Section 108(h)

[5] Copyright Act, Section 108(f)(3)

[6] Copyright Act, Section 108(b)

[7] Copyright Act, Section 108(c)

[8] Copyright Act, Section 108(g)(2)

[9] "Guidelines for the Proviso of Subsection 108(g)(2)," Section 1(a) in *House of Representatives Report No. 94-1476*, Section 108

[10] *Report of the Register of Copyrights: Library Reproduction of Copyrighted Works.* (17 *U.S.C.* 108) Washington D.C.: U.S. Government Printing Office, January 1983, p. 110

[11] Heller, J. and S.K. Wiant, *Copyright Handbook*, (AALL Publications Series), Littleton, CO: Fred B. Rothman Company, 1984, p. 28

[12]The full text of the guidelines appear in Appendix B.

[13]Copyright Act, Section 110(4)

[14]Full text of the guidelines is in Appendix C.

[15]Title 47, *U.S. Code*

[16]Title 47, *U.S. Code*, Section 605

[17]Copyright Act, Section 110(2)

[18]Copyright Act, Section 101

[19]For an interesting approach to obtaining licenses or permissions, see Mary Jo James, "Three Permission Surveys," in Jerome K. Miller and Others, *Video Copyright Permissions: A Guide to Securing Permission to Retain, Perform, and Transmit Television Programs Videotaped Off The Air* , (Friday Harbor, WA: Copyright Information Services, 1989), p. 73

[20]Copyright Act, Section 119(1)

[21]Copyright Act, Section 117, as amended by Public Law 96-517, December 2, 1980

[22]Full text of the ICC document appears in Appendix D

[23]Baumgarten, J. "Copyright and Computer Software Including Databases and Chip Technology," In M. Goldberg (ed), *Computer Software 1984: Protection and Marketing*, (New York: Practicing Law Institute, 1984), Vol I, p. 66

[24]Copyright Act, Section 106(4)

[25]Copyright Law, Section 110(1)

[26]U.S. Senate, *Report 94-473*, Section 107, p. 63

Chapter 3:

COPYRIGHT MANAGEMENT

If a copyright policy is to be effective, someone must manage the details and provide staff training. This is the duty of the Copyright Officer.

Copyright Officer:

The copyright officer is not a police officer, but is an information provider and a coordinator of copyright transactions. He or she should be a helper, not a threat. The faculty and staff should be encouraged to consult the copyright officer about all copyright matters. (The letter appointing a copyright officer appears in Appendix F; an announcement of the appointment appears in Appendix G.)

The copyright officer's responsibilities are:

1. Implement the Board Copyright Policy,

2. Establish and implement procedures to assure the institution and its employees comply with the copyright law,

3. Prepare and distribute a Faculty Copyright Manual,

4. Conduct training programs to inform the faculty about the copyright law and the institution's copyright policy,

5. Answer employees' questions about the copyright law,

6. Post appropriate copyright warning notices on copying equipment,

7. Stay abreast of new developments in the copyright law,

8. Negotiate licenses to copy, perform, or modify copyrighted works, and

9. Maintain records of permissions, licenses, etc.

Copyright Supervisors:

While compliance with the copyright institutional policy requires the cooperation of all employees, the copyright officer must be assisted by knowledgeable people in key positions. They include the directors of the library, media center, computer center, reprographics center, print shop, and media production facilities. These people frequently deal with requests for services and materials that involve copyrighted materials. These directors are expected to make copyright decisions on a daily basis. For this reason, they must learn about the areas of the copyright law that pertain to their responsibilities. They must work closely with the copyright officer to be sure the copyright law and the institution's Copyright Policy are observed.

Chapter 4:

COPYRIGHT QUICK GUIDE

The following "quick guide" is a brief summary of the copyright law for the faculty. It cannot substitute for a careful reading of the entire Faculty Copyright Manual. It is suggested that this be printed separately and distributed to the faculty as a pocket-sized, quick-reference tool. Footnotes have been omitted to keep it as brief as possible. The sources are cited elsewhere in this book.

I. Classroom Showing of Media Materials:

Films, videos, filmstrips, etc., whether purchased, rented or leased, may be shown in classrooms as part of the established curriculum. They may not be shown for recreational or entertainment without a "nontheatrical-public-performance license."

II. Duplicating Print Materials for Classroom Use:

A. An individual educator may make:

1. Single copies of:

a. chapter of a book,

b. an article from a magazine or newspaper,

c. a short story, short essay, or short poem, or

d. a chart, graph, diagram, drawing, cartoon or a picture from a book, magazine or newspaper.

2. Multiple copies for classroom use (not to exceed one copy per student per course):

a. a complete poem of less than 250 words,

b. an excerpt, not to exceed 250 words, from a longer poem,

c. a complete article, story or essay of less than 2,500 words,

d. an excerpt from a larger printed work not to exceed ten percent of the whole or 1,000 words,

e. one chart, graph, diagram, cartoon or picture per book or magazine issue if the individual item is not separately copyrighted, or

f. two pages or ten percent of the words from children's picture books or comic books.

3. All copies must include an appropriate copyright warning notice.

4. Copying must be made by the teacher or at the request of the teacher — not at the direction of higher authority.

B. An individual educator may not:

1. Copy more than one work or two excerpts from a single author during one class term,

2. Copy more than three works from a collective work or periodical volume during one class term,

3. Make multiple copies of more than nine works for distribution to students in one class term,

4. Use photocopies to create, replace, or substitute for an anthology,

5. Copy "consumable" works such as workbooks, standard tests, answer sheets, etc., or

6. Copy the same work from term to term without permission.

III. Library Reserve:

In lieu of classroom distribution, a reasonable number of copies may be placed on reserve for one semester. The number of copies depends on the size of the class, possibly one copy per ten students. Repeated use of a given material requires written permission.

IV. Music Copying:

   A. Sheet Music:

      1. An educator may:

         a. make an emergency copy for an imminent student performance, if the original copy was lost and there is not enough time to order a replacement copy. The temporary copy must be destroyed promptly after the performance,

         b. make multiple copies (up to one per student) of excerpts not constituting an entire performance unit or more than ten percent of the total work for academic purposes other than performance,

         c. edit or simplify purchased sheet music provided the character of the work is not distorted or lyrics added or altered, or

         d. duplicate individual parts if they are out of print or unavailable except in complete works and are used for teaching purposes.

      2. An educator may not:

         a. copy to substitute for an anthology or collection,

         b. copy from works intended to be "consumable,"

         c. copy for purposes of performance except for emergency copies to replace a lost copy (item IV.A.1.a above),

50

       d.   copy to substitute for purchase of music, or

       e.   copy without including the copyright notice.

  B.   Recordings:

      1.   An educator may make a single recording of student performances. The recording may be retained by the institution or the teacher for evaluation purposes only.

      2.   An educator may not reproduce musical recordings or convert them to another format (e.g., record to tape, tape to cassette, etc.) without written permission.

V. Recording Television Programs:

  A.   Recording Off the Air or Off the Cable:

      1.   The guidelines only apply to nonprofit institutions,

      2.   Television programs may be recorded from broadcast or simultaneous cable transmissions to the "general public," which excludes premium-pay programs, (e.g., HBO, CineMax, Disney, etc.),

      3.   Programs may be shown once and repeated once for reinforcement within ten "teaching days" of the broadcast. They may be retained for forty-five calendar days from the date of the broadcast,

      4.   Recording must be made by the teacher or at the request of the teacher,

      5.   Programs may not be rerecorded at a later date, regardless of the number of times it is rebroadcast,

6. A limited number of copies may be made to meet the needs of several teachers,

7. Programs need not be used in their entirety but may not be edited or electronically altered or combined,

8. All copies must include the copyright notice as it appears in the program, and

9. Institutions are expected to implement appropriate control procedures.

B. Recording Programs at Home for Classroom Use:

Television programs recorded at home by teachers may be used in the classroom if they meet all the conditions of the Recording Guidelines, noted in V.A, above.

C. Recording Public Broadcasting System Programs:

1. For short-term retention, follow the guidelines, in V.A, above.

2. For long-term retention, call the local PBS station for information about extended retention rights for specific programs.

D. Recording off of Satellites:

Programs may not be recorded from a television satellite unless the programs are authorized for free reception or the institution obtains a license to copy the programs.

E.   Transmission of Audiovisual Works:

Films, videos, etc. may not be transmitted to classrooms by open- or closed-circuit television without a transmission license or written permission.

F.   Home-Use-Only and Rental-Store Videos:

Programs labeled "For Home Use Only" or rented from rental stores may be used in classrooms under the following conditions:

1.   The programs are shown to students in a face-to-face setting,

2.   The programs are shown only in courses given for credit,

3.   The programs must be shown only in classrooms or other locations devoted to instruction,

4.   The programs must be legitimately-made copies, and

5.   The programs may not be shown for entertainment recreation, or reward.

VI. Computer Software and Databases:

A.   Backup copies:

One backup copy of computer software may be made for archival purposes in case the original is destroyed.

B.   Computer Laboratories:

Except for the back-up copy exemption above, software may not be duplicated without appropriate licenses or agreements.

C.   Multiple Loading:

Loading programs into several computers for simultaneous use is only permitted with permission or a license.

D.   Networks:

Computer software may not be used in a network (LAN or WAN) without permission or a license.

E.   Database Downloading:

Downloading from a database is an infringement. Short-term, single-use retention is "accepted" by the copyright owners as a fair use, but long-term retention and multiple use of data requires a license.

VII. Duplicating Films, Videotapes, Filmstrips, Slidesets, etc.

A.   An educator may duplicate a "small part" of an item for research or instruction. While no guidelines exist for copying these materials, the congressional reports accompanying the Copyright Revision Act of 1976 suggest that copying ten percent of a program is reasonable, if the ten percent is not the "essence" of the work.

B.   An educator may not:

1.   Reproduce an audiovisual work in its entirety, or

2.   Convert one media format into another, (e.g., film to video, filmstrip to slide, etc.), without permission.

VIII.   Microforms:

Microforms may be copied according to the rules applying to the materials reproduced, (e.g., books, periodicals, poetry, etc.). However, microform copies of works in the public domain may be copied freely.

IX. Newsletters:

Only a very small part of a newsletter may be duplicated without permission.

X. Artworks:

Artworks may not be duplicated without written permission except for illustrations copied under the "Agreement on Guidelines for Classroom Copying", (see II, A, above.)

XI. Electrocopying (Computer Scanning):

A.   Artworks: scanning for the purpose of reproduction or for creating derivative works requires permission.

B. Text:

1.   Scanning for research (e.g., textual analysis) is permissible, but

2.   Reproduction to create a copy or to prepare a derivative work requires permission.

XII. "Free and Benefit" Performances:

Storytelling, poetry readings, and musical performances of non-dramatic works are authorized if (a) admission is free, or (b) the gate receipts, over and above costs, go to a charitable cause, and the performers and managers contribute their services.

XIII. Student Projects:

Students may copy materials as a learning experience. This includes the right to integrate various materials into computer/sound/visual programs if the resultant product remains the property of the student, is not placed into the school's collection and no copies are sold, broadcast, transmitted, or performed outside the classroom.

Chapter 5:

OBTAINING PERMISSION

It is not difficult to request permission to duplicate or adopt copyrighted materials. Well-established procedures are available. For most materials, complete two copies of the request form shown in Appendix H and send it to the copyright owner. Complete information must be supplied before permission can be given. It is important to maintain orderly records of permissions sought, denied, or granted.

Permission to perform, broadcast, or transmit music is obtained from ASCAP, BMI, or SESAC. Their addresses appear in Appendix J.

Permission to retain programs recorded off the air is obtained from the Television Licensing Center (TLC), listed in Appendix J. If TLC cannot supply permission, permission must be obtained from the firm that produced the program, not the network.

Licenses to perform films and videos outside courses for credit are offered by Films, Inc., Swank Audio-Visuals, and the Motion Picture Licensing Corp. The addresses are in Appendix J.

Permission to copy computer software or use it on a network is obtained from the software publisher. Many software publishers sell a "site license" or "lab kit" to authorize making multiple copies of software or to authorize multiple loading.

Part III

ADOPTABLE
STUDENT COPYRIGHT MANUAL

by

Dr. Jerome K. Miller

Copyright laws were developed centuries ago to protect authors. If an author wrote a book, poem, or article he or she could register it with a government agency. That assured the author that others could not copy the work without permission. (Permission frequently included paying a fee.) If an author discovered that someone had copied the work without permission, he or she could sue the offender. If the author proved his or her case in court, judges frequently forced the offenders to pay for their mistakes.

The copyright law has changed over the centuries, but it still protects books, poems, maps, and magazine articles. Now, it also protects games, films, videos, computer programs, music videos, and other communication technologies.

Fair Use:

Today, the law also gives some rights to users, the ones who read books and watch videos. This "users right" started several centuries ago in England. People were being sued for copyright infringements for copying short quotations. At one point, an author could be sued — and loose — for copying one sentence without permission. The judges decided the law had gone too far so they began finding some defendants innocent on the basis of "fair quotation." The judges said it was not illegal to include short quotations in a book or article, so long as the quotation was brief.

U.S. judges began applying "fair quotation," but they called it "fair use." Whatever it is called, "fair quotation" or "fair use" is the right of an individual to quote a small part of a copyrighted work without asking permission or paying a fee.

When the U.S. copyright law was revised in 1976, it included a "fair use" section. The teachers' associations lobbied heavily for a "fair use" exemption authorizing teachers to copy for classroom use. The 1976 copyright law and the related documents include specific exemptions authorizing teachers to copy pages from books, encyclopedias, and magazines to distribute to their students. It also authorizes teachers to videotape programs off the air for classroom use. Congress did not give teachers a "blank check" to copy everything. Some restrictions apply to copying by teachers.

Unfortunately, the new copyright law did not include a specific exemption for copying by students. However, the fair use exemption in the law applies to students. In applying "fair use," it is important to apply the "injury test." Most authors are poorly paid for their work, so copying which deprives them of part of their income is "injurious" to them. Copying a few pages from a book probably does not "injure" the author. On the other hand, copying an entire book to avoid buying it deprives the author of income from the sale of that book. In that case, the copying is "injurious," and illegal.

Students are most likely to injure copyright owners by copying computer software, records, cassettes, and videos. Copying software, records, cassettes, or videos to avoid buying them injures many people. The royalties from music, videos, and software are shared by many people, including composers, musicians, and technicians. The loss of income from the sale of software, videos, records, and cassettes does injure these people. Therefore copying these items to avoid buying them is both "injurious," and illegal.

Copying to complete an assignment:

Students in computer classes often enter text, data, illustrations or logorithims as part of a class requirement. Students producing media projects (slides, film, video, etc.) often copy pictures from books, scenes from videos or TV programs, or music from records. In most cases, this appears to be a legitimate application of "fair use."

When Congress rewrote the copyright law, it stated that copying by students as a "learning exercise" was a "fair use." If you copy pictures, music, or text to produce a media project, that copying may be a "fair use" as long as the copy is only used for a school project. You may submit the project for a grade and the teacher may show it in class. That much is probably a "fair use."

The key question concerns future uses of the material you produce for class assignments. You may keep it for your own enjoyment and you probably can show it to a prospective employer during a job interview. However, if it includes copies of copyrighted works, it is probably illegal to share a computer program on a bulletin board or to exchange it with friends. In the case of media productions, it may be illegal for you to show it to an audience. It is particularly important that you not broadcast the program or transmit it though a cable system without checking on copyright permissions. Your school Copyright Officer can help you decide if you must request permission for the items you copied. If the only thing you copied is music, the station or cable system's licenses may cover the music — but verify that before the broadcast or cable transmission.

Please remember, your education would not be possible without books, magazines, encyclopedias, computer programs, videos, and the like. You benefit from the creative efforts of others. Those who created those materials are entitled to a decent income from their labor. Copying more than a small part of a copyrighted work denies them of a fair return on their labor. It does not seem fair, and it is clearly illegal.

APPENDICES

A: Agreement on Guidelines for Classroom Copying
    in Not-for-Profit Educational Institutions With
    Respect to Books and Periodicals 65

B: Guidelines for Educational Uses of Music 71

C: Guidelines for Off-Air Recording of Broadcast
    Programming for Educational Purposes 75

D: International Council for Computers in Education
    Suggested Software Use Guidelines 79

E: CONTU Guidelines for Interlibrary Loans 87

F: Appointment of an Institutional Copyright Officer . . .91

G: Letter Informing Faculty of the Copyright Officer
    Appointment 93

H: Permission Request Form 95

I: Request for Off-Air Taping 97

J: Selected Addresses 99

K: Selected Passages from the Copyright Law 103

Appendix A

AGREEMENT ON GUIDELINES FOR CLASSROOM COPYING IN NOT FOR PROFIT EDUCATIONAL INSTITUTIONS WITH RESPECT TO BOOKS AND PERIODICALS

In a joint letter to Chairman Kastenmeier, dated March 19, 1976, the representatives of the Ad Hoc Committee of Educational Institutions and Organizations on Copyright Law Revision, and of the Authors League of America, Inc., and the Association of American Publishers, Inc., stated:

You may remember that in our letter of March 8, 1976 we told you that the negotiating teams representing authors and publishers and the Ad Hoc Group had reached tentative agreement on guidelines to insert in the Committee Report covering educational copying from books and periodicals under Section 107 of H.R. 2223 and S. 22, and that as part of that tentative agreement each side would accept the amendments to Sections

107 and 504 which were adopted by your Subcommittee on March 3, 1976.

We are now happy to tell you that the agreement has been approved by the principals and we enclose a copy herewith. We had originally intended to translate the agreement into language suitable for inclusion in the legislative report dealing with Section 107, but we have since been advised by committee staff that this will not be necessary.

As stated above, the agreement refers only to copying from books and periodicals, and it is not intended to apply to musical or audiovisual works.

The full text of the agreement is as follows:

The purpose of the following guidelines is to state the minimum and not the maximum standards of educational fair use under Section 107 of H.R. 2223. The parties agree that the conditions determining the extent of permissible copying for educational purposes may change in the future; that certain types of copying permitted under these guidelines may not be permissible in the future; and conversely that in the future other types of copying not permitted under these guidelines may be permissible under revised guidelines.

Moreover, the following statement of guidelines is not intended to limit the types of copying permitted under the standards of fair use under judicial decision and which are stated in Section 107 of the Copyright Revision Bill. There may be instances in which copying which does not fall within the guidelines stated below may nonetheless be permitted under the criteria of fair use.

GUIDELINES

I. Single Copying for Teachers

A single copy may be made of any of the following by or for a teacher at his or her individual request for his or her scholarly research or use in teaching or preparation to teach a class:

    A. A chapter from a book;

    B. An article from a periodical or newspaper;

    C. A short story, short essay or short poem,
        whether or not from a collective work;

    D. A chart, graph, diagram, drawing,
        cartoon or picture from a book, periodical,
        or newspaper.

II. Multiple Copies for Classroom Use

Multiple copies (not to exceed in any event more than one copy per pupil in a course) may be made by or for the teacher giving the course for classroom use or discussion; provided that:

    A. The copying meets the tests of brevity and
        spontaneity as defined below; and,

    B. Mets the cumulative effect test as defined
        below; and,

    C. Each copy includes a notice of copyright.

67

Definitions

Brevity

(i)Poetry: (a) A complete poem if less than 250 words and if printed on not more than two pages or, (b) from a longer poem, an excerpt of not more than 250 words.

(ii) Prose: (a) Either a complete article, story or essay of less than 2,500 words, or (b) an excerpt from any prose work of not more than 1,000 words or 10% of the work, whichever is less, but in any event a minimum of 500 words.

[Each of the numerical limits stated in "i" and "ii" above may be expanded to permit the completion of an unfinished line of a poem or of an unfinished prose paragraph.]

(iii) Illustration: One chart, graph, diagram, drawing, cartoon or picture per book or per periodical issue.

(iv) "Special" works: Certain works in poetry, prose or in "poetic prose" which often combine language with illustrations and which are intended sometimes for children and at other times for a more general audience fall short of 2,500 words in their entirety. Paragraph "ii" above notwithstanding such "special works" may not be reproduced in their entirety; however, an excerpt comprising not more than two of the published pages of such special work and containing not more then 10% of the words found in the text thereof, may be reproduced.

Spontaneity

(i) The copying is at the instance and inspiration of the individual teacher, and

(ii) The inspiration and decision to use the work and the moment of its use for maximum teaching effectiveness are so close in time that it would be unreasonable to expect a timely reply to a request for permission.

Cumulative Effect

(i) The copying of the material is for only one course in the school in which the copies are made.

(ii) Not more than one short poem, article, story, essay or two excerpts may be copied from the same author, nor more than three from the same collective work or periodical volume during one class term.

(iii) There shall not be more than nine instances of such multiple copying for one course during one class term.

[The limitations stated in "ii" and "iii" above shall not apply to current news periodicals and newspapers and current news sections of other periodicals.]

III.   Prohibitions as to I and II Above

Notwithstanding any of the above, the following shall be prohibited:

(A) Copying shall not be used to create or to replace or substitute for anthologies, compilations or collective works. Such replacement or substitution may occur whether copies of various works or excerpts therefrom are accumulated or reproduced and used separately.

(B) There shall be no copying of or from works intended to be "consumable" in the course of study or of teaching. These include workbooks, exercises, standardized tests and test booklets and answer sheets and like consumable materials.

(C) Copying shall not:

    (a)   substitute for the purchase of books, publishers' reprints or periodicals;

    (b)   be directed by higher authority;

    (c)   be repeated with respect to the same item by the same teacher from term to term.

(D) No charge shall be made to the student beyond the actual cost of the photocopying.

Agreed March 19, 1976.

Ad Hoc Committee on Copyright Law Revision:

By SHELDON ELLIOTT STEINBACH.

Author-Publisher Group:

Authors League of America: By IRWIN KARP, Counsel.

Association of American Publishers, Inc.: By ALEXANDER C. HOFFMAN, Chairman, Copyright Committee.

Appendix B

GUIDELINES FOR EDUCATIONAL USE OF MUSIC

In a joint letter dated April 30, 1976, representatives of the Music Publishers' Association of the United States, Inc., the National Music Publishers' Association, Inc., the Music Teachers National Association, the Music Educators' National Conference, the National Association of Schools of Music, and the Ad Hoc Committee on Copyright Law Revision, wrote to Chairman Kastenmeier as follows:

During the hearings on H.R. 2223 in June 1975, you and several of your subcommittee members suggested that concerned groups should work together in developing guidelines which would be helpful to clarify Section 107 of the bill.

Representatives of music educators and music publishers delayed their meetings until guidelines had been developed relative to books and periodicals. Shortly after that work was completed and those guidelines were forwarded to your subcommittee, representatives of the undersigned music organizations met together with representatives of the Ad Hoc

71

Committee on Copyright Law Revision to draft guidelines relative to music.

We are very pleased to inform you that the discussions thus have been fruitful on the guidelines which have been developed. Since private music teachers are an important factor in music education, due consideration has been given to the concerns of that group.

We trust that this will be helpful in the report on the bill to clarify Fair Use as it applies to music.

The text of the guidelines accompanying this letter is as follows:

The purpose of the following guidelines is to state the minimum and not the maximum standards of educational fair use under Section 107 of HR 2223. The parties agree that the conditions determining the extent of permissible copying for educational purposes may change in the future; that certain types of copying permitted under these guidelines may not be permissible in the future, the conversely that in the future other types of copying not permitted under these guidelines may be permissible under revised guidelines.

Moreover, the following statement of guidelines is not intended to limit the types of copying permitted under the standards of fair use under judicial decision and which are stated in Section 107 of the Copyright Revision Bill. There may be instances in which copying which does not fall within the guidelines stated below may nonetheless be permitted under the criteria of fair use.

A. Permissible Uses

1. Emergency copying to replace purchased copies which for any reason are not available for an imminent performance

provided purchased replacement copies shall be substituted in due course.

2. For academic purposes other than performance, single or multiple copies of excerpts of works may be made, provided that the excerpts do not comprise a part of the whole which would constitute a performable unit such as a selection, movement or aria, but in no case more than 10% of the whole work. The number of copies shall not exceed one copy per pupil.[1]

3. Printed copies which have been purchased may be edited or simplified provided that the fundamental character of the work is not distorted or the lyrics, if any, altered or lyrics added if none exist.

4. A single copy of recordings of performances by students may be made for evaluation or rehearsal purposes and may be retained by the educational institution or individual teacher.

5. A single copy of a sound recording (such as a tape, disk or cassette) of copyrighted music may be made from sound recordings owned by an educational institution or an individual teacher for the purpose of constructing aural exercises or examinations and may be retained by the educational institution or individual teacher. (This pertains only to the copyright of the music itself and not to any copyright which may exist in the sound recording.)

B. Prohibitions

1. Copying to create or replace or substitute for anthologies, compilations or collective works.

2. Copying of or from works intended to be "consumable" in the course of study or of teaching such as workbooks, exercises, standardized tests and answer sheets and like material.

3. Copying for the purpose of performance, except as in A(1) above.

4. Copying for the purpose of substituting for the purchase of music, except as in A(1) and A(2) above.

5. Copying without inclusion of the copyright notice which appears on the printed copy.

NOTES

[1] Section A(2) was revised at the last moment, at the request of the joint committee that prepared the guidelines. The original text of Section 2 consisted of two parts. Part 2 (a) was redesignated in the final text as Part 2, as it appears near the top of the preceding page. Part 2 (b) of the orginal text was deleted. The deleted text read:

"(b) For academic purposes other than performance, a single copy of an entire performable unit (section, movement, aria, etc.) that is, (1) confirmed by the copyright proprietor to be out of print or (2) unavailable except in a larger work, may be made by or for a teacher solely for the purpose of his or her scholarly research or in preparation to teach a class."

Appendix C

GUIDELINES FOR OFF-AIR RECORDING OF BROADCAST PROGRAMMING FOR EDUCATIONAL PURPOSES

In March of 1979, Congressman Robert Kastenmeier, chairman of the House Subcommittee on Courts, Civil Liberties, and Administration of Justice, appointed a Negotiating Committee consisting of representatives of education organizations, copyright proprietors, and creative guilds and unions. The following guidelines reflect the Negotiating Committee's consensus as to the application of "fair use" to the recording, retention, and use of television broadcast programs for educational purposes. They specify periods of retention and use of such off-air recordings in classrooms and similar places devoted to instruction and for homebound instruction. The purpose of establishing these guidelines is to provide standards for both owners and users of copyrighted television programs.

1. The guidelines were developed to apply only to off-air recording by nonprofit educational institutions.

2. A broadcast program may be recorded off-air simultaneously with broadcast transmission (including simultaneous cable retransmission) and retained by a nonprofit educational institution for a period not to exceed the first forty-five (45) consecutive calendar days after date of recording. Upon conclusion of such retention period, all off-air recordings must be erased or destroyed immediately. "Broadcast programs" are television programs transmitted by television stations for reception by the general public without charge.

3. Off-air recordings may be used once by individual teachers in the course of relevant teaching activities, and repeated once only when instructional reinforcement is necessary, in classrooms and similar places devoted to instruction within a single building, cluster or campus, as well as in the homes of students receiving formalized home instruction, during the first ten (10) consecutive school days in the forty-five (45) day calendar day retention period. "School days" are school session days — not counting weekends, holidays, vacations, examination periods, and other scheduled interruptions — within the forty-five (45) calendar day retention period.

4. Off-air recordings may be made only at the request of and used by individual teachers, and may not be regularly recorded in anticipation of requests. No broadcast program may be recorded off-air more than once at the request of the same teacher, regardless of the number of times the program may be broadcast.

5. A limited number of copies may be reproduced from each off-air recording to meet the legitimate needs of teachers under these guidelines. Each such additional copy shall be subject to all provision governing the original recording.

6. After the first ten (10) consecutive school days, off-air recordings may be used up to the end of the forty-five (45) calendar day retention period only for teacher evaluation purposes i.e., to determine whether or not to include the broadcast program in the teaching curriculum, and may not be used in the recording institution for student exhibition or any other non-evaluation purpose without authorization.

7. Off-air recordings need not be used in their entirety, but the recorded programs may not be altered from their original content. Off-air recordings may not be physically or electronically combined or merged to constitute teaching anthologies or compilations.

8. All copies of off-air recording must include the copyright notice on the broadcast program as recorded.

9. Educational institutions are expected to establish appropriate control procedures to maintain the integrity of these guidelines.

Appendix D

INTERNATIONAL COUNCIL FOR COMPUTERS IN EDUCATION (ICCE) SUGGESTED SOFTWARE USE GUIDELINES

Background:

During 1982-83, educators, software developers, and hardware and software vendors cooperated to develop the *ICCE Policy Statement on Network and Multiple Machine Software.* This Policy Statement was adopted by the Board of Directors of the International Council for Computers in Education (ICCE) in 1983, and was published and distributed. It has received support from hardware and software vendors, industry associations and other education associations. One component of the Policy Statement, the "Model District Policy on Software Copyright," has been adopted by school districts throughout the world.

Now, three years later, as the educational computer market has changed and the software market has matured, ICCE has responded to suggestions that the policy statement be reviewed by a new committee and revisions be made to reflect the changes that have taken place both in the market place and in the schools.

The 1986-87 ICCE Software Copyright Committee is composed of educators, industry associations, hardware vendors, software developers and vendors, and lawyers. All the participants of this new Committee agree that the educational market should be served by developers and preserved by educators. To do so requires that the ICCE Policy Statement be revisited every few years while the industry and the use of computers in education are still developing.

Responsibilities:

In the previous Policy Statement, lists of responsibilities were assigned to appropriate groups: educators; hardware vendors; and software developers and vendors. The suggestion that school boards show their responsibility by approving a district copyright policy was met with enthusiasm, and many districts approved a policy based on the ICCE Model Policy. The suggestion that software vendors adopt multiple-copy discounts and offer lab packs to schools was likewise well received; many educational software publishers now offer such pricing. It is therefore the opinion of this committee that, for the most part, the 1983 list of recommendations has become a fait accompli within the industry, and to repeat it here would be an unnecessary redundancy.

Nevertheless, the Committee does suggest that all parties involved in the educational computing market be aware of what the other parties are doing to preserve this market, and that the following three recommendations be considered for adoption by the appropriate agencies.

School District Copyright Policy:

The Committee recommends that school districts approve a District Copyright Policy that includes both computer software and other media. A Model District Policy on Software Copyright is enclosed.

Particular attention should be directed to item five, recommending that *only one* person in the district be given the authority to sign software licensing agreements. This implies that such a person should become familiar with licensing and purchasing rights of all copyrighted materials.

Suggested Software Use Guidelines:

In the absence of clear legislation, legal opinion or case law, it is suggested that school districts adopt the enclosed Suggested Software Use Guidelines as guidelines for software use within the district. The recommendation of Guidelines is similar to the situation currently used by many education agencies for off-air video recording. While these Guidelines do not carry the force of law, they do represent the collected opinion on fair software use for nonprofit education agencies from a variety of experts in the software copyright field.

Copyright Page Recommendations:

The Committee recommends that educators look to the copyright page of software documentation to find their rights, obligations and license restrictions regarding an individual piece of software.

The Committee also suggests that software publishers use the documentation copyright page to *clearly* delineate the users' (owners' or licensees') rights in at least these five areas:

1. How is a back-up copy made or obtained, how many are allowed, and how are the back-ups to be used (e.g., not to be used on a second machine at the same time)?

2. Is it permissible to load the disk(s) into multiple computers for use at the same time?

3. Is it permissible to use the software on a local area network, and will the company support such use? Or is a network version available from the publisher?

4. Are lab packs or quantity discounts available from the publisher?

5. Is it permissible for the owner or licensee to make copies of the printed documentation? or are additional copies available, and how?

ICCE — Suggested Software Use Guidelines

The 1976 U.S. Copyright Act and its 1980 Amendments remain vague in some areas of software use and its application to education. Where the law itself is vague, software licenses tend to be much more specific. It is therefore imperative that educators read the software's copyright page and understand the licensing restrictions printed there. If these uses are not addressed, the following Guidelines are recommended.

These Guidelines do not have the force of law, but they do represent the collected opinion on fair software use by nonprofit educational agencies from a variety of experts in the software copyright field.

Back-up Copy: The Copyright Act is clear in permitting the owner of software a back-up copy of the software to be held for use as an archival copy in the event the original disk fails to function. Such back-up copies are not to be used on a second computer at the same time the original is in use.

Multiple-loading: The Copyright Act is most unclear as it applies to loading the contents of one disk into multiple computers for use at the same time. In the absence of a license expressly permitting the user to load the contents of one disk into many computers for use at the same time, it is suggested that you not allow this activity to take place. The fact that you physically can do so is irrelevant. In an effort to make it easier for schools to buy software for each computer station, many software publishers offer lab packs and other quantity buying incentives. Contact individual publishers for details.

Local Area Network Software Use: It is suggested that before placing a software program on a local area network or disk-sharing system for use by multiple users at the same time, you obtain a written license agreement from the copyright holder giving you permission to do so. The fact that you are able to physically load the program on the network is, again, irrelevant. You should obtain a license permitting you to do so before you act.

Model District Policy on Software Copyright

It is the intent of [district] to adhere to the provisions of copyright laws in the area of microcomputer software. It is also the intent of the district to comply with the license agreements and/or policy statements contained in the software packages used in the district. In circumstances where the interpretation of the copyright law is ambiguous, the district shall look to the applicable license agreement to determine appropriate use of the software (or the district will abide by the approved Software Use Guidelines).

We recognize that computer software piracy is a major problem for the industry and that violations of copyright laws contribute to higher costs and greater efforts to prevent copying and/or lessen incentives for the development of effective educational uses of microcomputers. Therefore, in an effort to discourage violation of copyright laws and to prevent such illegal activities:

1. The ethical and practical implications of software piracy will be taught to educators and school children in all schools in the district (e.g., covered in fifth grade social studies classes).

2. District employees will be informed that they are expected to adhere to section 117 of the 1976 Copyright Act as amended in 1980, governing the use of software (e.g., each building principle will devote one faculty meeting to the subject each year).

3. When permission is obtained from the copyright holder to use software on a disk-sharing system, efforts will be made to secure this software from copying.

4. Under no circumstances shall illegal copies of copyrighted software be made or used on school equipment.

5. [Name or job title] of this school district is designated as the only individual who may sign license agreements for software for schools in the district. Each school using licensed software should have a signed copy of the software agreement.

6. The principal at each school site is responsible for establishing practices which will enforce this district copyright policy at the school level.

The Board of Directors of the International Council for Computers in Education approved this policy statement January,

1987. The members of the 1986 ICCE Software Copyright Committee are:

Sueann Ambron, American Association of Publishers
Gary Becker, Seminole Co. Public Schools, Florida
Daniel T. Brooks, Cadwalader, Wickersham & Taft
LeRoy Finkel, International Council for Computers in Education
Virginia Helm, Western Illinois University
Kent Kehrberg, Minnesota Educational Computing Corp.
Dan Kunz, Commodore Business Machines
Bodie Marx, Mindscape, Inc.
Kenton Pattie, International Communications Industries Assn.
Carol Risher, American Association of Publishers
Linda Roberts, US Congress, Office of Technology Assessment
Donald A. Ross, Microcomputer Workshops Courseware
Larry Smith, Wayne County Intermediate School Dist., Michigan
Ken Wasch, Software Publishers' Association

For more information write to the ICCE Software Copyright Committee, ICCE, University of Oregon, 1787 Agate St., Eugene, OR 97403.

Appendix E:

CONTU GUIDELINES FOR INTERLIBRARY LOANS

Guidelines for the proviso of Subsection 108(g)(2), Photocopying.

1. As used in the proviso of subsection 108(g)(2), the words, "... such aggregate quantities as to substitute for a subscription or purchase of such work" shall mean:

(a) with respect to any given periodical (as opposed to any given issue of a periodical), filled requests of a library or archives (a "requesting entity") within any calendar year for a total of six or more copies of an article or articles published in such periodical within five years prior to the date of the request. These guidelines specifically shall not apply, directly or indirectly, to any request of a requesting entity for a copy or copies of an article or articles published in any issue of a periodical, the publication date of which is more than five years prior to the date when the request is made. These guidelines do not define the meaning, with respect to such a request, of "... such aggregate quantities as to substitute for a subscription to (such periodical)"

(b) With respect to any other material described in subsection 108(d), (including fiction or poetry), filled requests of a requesting entity within any calendar year for a total of six or more copies of phonorecords or from any given work (including a collective work) during the entire period when such material shall be protected by copyright.

2. In the event that a requesting entity

(a) shall have in force or shall have entered an order for a subscription to a periodical, or

(b) has within its collection, or shall have entered an order for a copy or phonorecord of any other copyrighted work, material from either category of which it desires to obtain by copy from another library or archives (the "supplying entity"), because the material to be copied is not reasonably available for use by the requesting entity itself, then the fulfillment of such request shall be treated as though the requesting entity made such copy from its own collection. A library or archives may request a copy or phonorecord from a supplying entity only under those circumstances where the requesting entity would have been able, under the provisions of section 108, to supply such copy from materials in its own collection.

3. No request for a copy or phonorecord of any material to which these guidelines apply may be fulfilled by the supplying entity unless such request is accompanied by a representation by the requesting entity that the request was made in conformity with these guidelines.

4. The requesting entity shall maintain records of all requests made by it for copies or phonorecords of any materials to which these guideline apply and shall maintain records of the fulfillment of such requests, which records shall be retained until the end of the third complete calendar year after the end of the

calendar year in which the respective request shall have been made.

5. As part of the review provided for in subsection 108(i), these guidelines shall be reviewed not later than five years from the effective date of this bill.

Appendix F

APPOINTMENT OF
AN INSTITUTIONAL
COPYRIGHT OFFICER

(Letterhead)

(date)

(Name of institution) intends to adhere to the U.S. Copyright Law (Title 17, *U.S. Code*, Sect. 101, et. seq.).

To facilitate the observance of the copyright law (name of person) is hereby named as the institution's Copyright Officer, effective (date).

The copyright officer shall:

1. implement the (name of institution) Board Copyright Policy,

2. prepare and distribute a Faculty Copyright Manual,

3. establish and implement procedures to assure that the institution and it's employees are in compliance with the copyright law,

4. conduct copyright training programs to inform employees of the copyright law and the institutions copyright policy to enable them to perform their duties within the intent of the law and the policy, and

5. maintain appropriate records of permissions, purchase agreements, and licenses.

Signed:

Appendix G:

LETTER INFORMING THE FACULTY OF THE APPOINTMENT OF A COPYRIGHT OFFICER

On (date), (name of copyright officer) was appointed as the institution's Copyright Officer.

He/She may be reached at (address and telephone number).

The Copyright Officer is not a police officer but is a source of information about the copyright law. He/she will offer a series of workshops so the faculty is informed about the copyright law. The copyright officer assists the faculty and the administration in complying with the law and should be considered as a helper and not a threat. The faculty and staff are encouraged to ask the copyright officer questions about the copyright law.

The Copyright Officer shall:

1. implement the Board Copyright Policy (copy attached),

2. prepare and distribute a Faculty Copyright Manual,

3. conduct copyright training programs to inform its faculty about the copyright law and the institution's copyright policy,

4. answer employee questions related to the copyright law,

5. post appropriate copyright warning notices on copying equipment,

6. stay abreast of changes in the copyright law to keep the administration and employees informed,

7. negotiate for permissions and licenses to duplicate, perform, or adopt copyrighted materials, and

8. maintain appropriate records of permissions and licenses.

Signed:

Appendix H:

PERMISSION REQUEST FORM

(Institutional letterhead)
(date)

(Name and address)

Dear Sir/Madam:

Please may I/we have permission to copy the following:

1. Work: (author, title, edition, and date)

2. Pages: (list pages to be copied)

3. Copying method: (photocopy, transfer to slides, etc.)

4. Number of copies:

5. Use of copies: (distribution to students, incorporated in a book, etc.)

6. Distribution: (class handout, shown in class, etc.)

7. Cost to audience: (distributed free, etc.)

8. Type of copy: (photocopy, printout, slide, etc.)

9. Modifications: (if any)

10. Intended date of use:

Enclosed is a photocopy of the material requested.

Two copies of this form are being sent. If you will grant permission, please check the appropriate box, sign, and return one copy to me. The other copy can be retained for your files.

Thank you.

Sincerely,

(Signature)
(Name typed)
(Title)

☐ Permission granted as per request

☐ Permission denied.

Conditions if any:

Signature:
Title:
Date:

Appendix I:

REQUEST FOR OFF-AIR TAPING

The "Guidelines for Off-Air Recording of Broadcast Programming for Education Purposes" requires that records be maintained to assure that the conditions in the fair-use guidelines are observed. The following information is necessary to assure that the institution complies with the criteria. Please complete all the information and return the form to the Copyright Officer.

Instructor:

School/Department:

Class:

PROGRAM RECORDED AT SCHOOL

Title of Program:

Station or Channel: Length of Program:

Date Recorded: Date of Use:

Required Erase Date: Date Erased:

PROGRAM RECORDED AT HOME

Title of Program:

Station or Channel: Length of Program:

Date Recorded: Date of Use:

Required Erase Date: Date Erased:

Would you recommend this material for purchase, lease or license?

☐   Highly Recommended   ☐   Recommended
☐   Not Recommended

How many times would you use this program each year?_____

The Fair Use Guidelines are summarized on the back of this form. (See Chapter 4, Part V.)

(Signature)